Smugg
Dorset

by Robert Westwood

ISBN 978-0-9552061-4-6

First published in 2007 by:
Inspiring Places Publishing
2 Down Lodge Close
Alderholt
Fordingbridge
Hants.
SP63JA
robert.westwood3@btinternet.com
www.inspiringplaces.co.uk

Printed by ACH Colour, Bournemouth

Contents

Page

Other books from *Inspiring Places Publishing:*

Fossils and Rocks of the Jurassic Coast
Ancient Dorset
Day Tours in the East of Dorset
Alien Big Cats of Dorset
Dark Age Dorset
Mysterious Places of Dorset

Check out the image galleries and buy books and prints on line at:
www.inspiringplaces.co.uk
First page: Kimmeridge Bay

Front cover: Looking westwards from Durdle Door towards Swyre Head and Bat's Head where the cave was a favourite smugglers' hideout.

Rear cover: Worbarrow Bay, scene of many a landing by smugglers and the site of a ghostly legend of a drowned smuggler.

Introduction

What do you know of the "golden age" of smuggling? Have you ever thought as you walked along Smugglers' Lane, enjoyed a drink at the Smugglers' Inn or watched the sea at Brandy Bay what it was like along Dorset's beautiful coast as gangs of smugglers and the Riding Officers of the Revenue Service went about their conflicting business as perpetrators and preventers of what was a huge national business? Perhaps your perception is summed up by this extract from Rudyard Kipling's well known poem "A Smuggler's Song".

If you wake at midnight, and hear a horse's feet,
Don't go drawing back the blind, or looking in the street,
Them that ask no questions isn't told a lie.
Watch the wall my darling while the Gentlemen go by.
Five and twenty ponies,
Trotting through the dark -
Brandy for the Parson, 'Baccy for the Clerk.
Laces for a lady; letters for a spy,
Watch the wall my darling while the Gentlemen go by!
Running round the woodlump if you chance to find
Little barrels, roped and tarred, all full of brandy-wine,
Don't you shout to come and look, nor use 'em for your play.
Put the brishwood back again - and they'll be gone next day !

Above: The New Forest - ideal for convoys carrying contraband!

If you see the stable-door setting open wide;
If you see a tired horse lying down inside;
If your mother mends a coat cut about and tore;
If the lining's wet and warm - don't you ask no more !
If you meet King George's men, dressed in blue and red,
You be careful what you say, and mindful what is said.
If they call you " pretty maid," and chuck you 'neath the chin,
Don't you tell where no one is, nor yet where no one's been !
Knocks and footsteps round the house - whistles after dark -
You've no call for running out till the house-dogs bark.

Few areas of the south coast do not have their own smuggling tales and legends. The clandestine activities of smugglers in the 18th and early 19th centuries have entered popular imagination as exciting and often wholesome adventures. People then and now, it seems, had or have little sympathy for the cheated government whose crippling taxation and other policies condemned the rural poor to live in abject misery - were it not for the heroic smugglers. Is this an accurate perception, or like other organised crime, was smuggling in reality a nasty business perpetrated by vicious thugs? Perhaps there is truth in both sides of the coin; as Kipling's poem suggests, all levels of society could be involved from the *parson* to the *clerk* and there is no doubt that most ordinary people would not have betrayed the smugglers to the authorities, even without any intimidation.

Smuggling only became a worthwhile occupation when tax or duty was placed on the movement of goods. If something could be imported or exported without paying duty then a good profit could be made. Customers as well as smugglers stood to benefit.

Around the year 1300 Edward I decided he could raise some extra taxes by putting a duty on the sale of wool, England's most important export. Rather than tax it at source, it seemed a simple way was to collect the tax as ships entered and left port. Of course, people who resented paying the tax soon found ways round this and as the Hundred Years War dragged on, more money was needed and taxes went up; so smuggling became more rewarding and grew in scale.

Relatively small scale smuggling went on for centuries but during the Civil War a new tax was invented that was to herald a huge expansion of the smuggling "industry": this was an excise tax on essential commodities. In addition, common lands used for hunting by peasants were enclosed and hunting by common people was banned. These measures had a devastating impact on the rural poor. In the 18th century excise taxes were expanded and increased as the need to pay for more wars grew. For many poor people the solution to their troubles was obvious. By 1783 it was estimated that nine out of ten families supported smuggling and every level of society was involved. With an old and creaking system of customs houses to collect the duties it was a relatively simple matter to smuggle goods in and out of the country. This and the huge public resentment of crippling taxation was to set the scene for an episode of history that would be romanticised in the imaginations of future generations.

Above: A Revenue cutter chases a smugglers' lugger.
© Richard Platt "Smugglers' Britain" 2006

Smuggling Methods

In the 18th and early 19th century smuggling developed into a huge industry. For this to have happened common sense tells us that it must have been profitable and that it must have been relatively easy to do. It was, after all, against the law and punishments were severe. Of course, the hardships that were endured, particularly by the rural poor, were a huge motivating factor.

So what made it possible for large numbers of people to engage in this activity with little fear of reprisal? One thing was the lack of law enforcement. At the end of the 17th century a corps of "Riding Officers" was set up to patrol the southern coastline. Around 300 were employed, a pitifully inadequate number to guard the many hundreds of miles of shoreline around the clock. During the course of the 18th century new laws were passed to combat the increasing smuggling activity but proved largely ineffective. Stronger sentences for smuggling merely resulted in the increased use of violence by smugglers. In 1733 an excise bill was introduced by Robert Walpole which sought to remove some of the customs duties from certain imports and collect them inland. This would have reduced profits for smugglers. However, because it would have required greater powers of search by Revenue officers it was widely opposed and he was forced to drop the bill.

Below: The coast path near Kimmeridge, made to aid Riding Officers.

Above: Worbarrow Bay, a favourite landing spot for smugglers.

The government tried offering free pardons to smugglers who turned informant, but this also failed as the majority of smugglers lived in communities where many were involved and retribution from former comrades was the greater fear.

As the century progressed more draconian laws were passed. In 1746 the sentence for harbouring a smuggler was now death and whole communities could be fined for offences. However, the American War of Independence drained much manpower from the armed services and this left few to help the Revenue men.

When we take into account the conditions of the rural poor and the steadily increasing tax burden that ordinary people were subjected to, we can see why, during the 18th century, smuggling became a way of life for whole communities and its impact stretched far inland from the coves, beaches and inlets where the goods were landed. Some facts and figures help us to appreciate the scale of smuggling operations. In 1719 it was recorded that 5 ships unloaded their illicit cargoes at Worbarrow Bay at one time. Smuggling trips frequently brought in several thousand gallons of spirits. Imagine having to organise the concealment, transport and distribution of over a thousand barrels! It has been estimated that, at one time, approximately four fifths of the tea drunk in England had not had duty paid on it.

The methods used by 18th century smugglers have passed into folklore and many towns and villages along Britain's southern coast have smuggling tales associated with them and local names derived from smuggling activities. Thomas Hardy's short story "The Distracted Preacher" is an excellent guide to the refinement of methods used in smuggling's heyday. Although writing at a time when smuggling had greatly declined due to government initiatives [finally!], Hardy nevertheless knew a lot about this illegal activity from people who had been involved with it, including his own grandfather, whom he recalls taking kegs of whisky from men who called in the middle of the night.

Set in the early 19th century when smuggling was about to be brought under control, the story concerns a visiting preacher who falls for a young widow who is one of the chief organisers of the local smuggling enterprise. As the preacher eventually realises, almost everyone in the village is involved, it is highly organised and the danger from the Revenue men easily avoided. Barrels of spirit are unloaded from ships at pre-arranged locations. If there is any danger of being discovered, ships are warned off by lighting beacons on headlands. The whole thing is done at the dead of night and on evenings without a moon. The barrels are hidden in a variety of ingenious locations, including the church and a secret cavity under a tree.

The cargoes are paid for beforehand and the men who unload and carry are also paid in advance. The young widow and her "business" partner make their money from the subsequent sale of the spirits. They are also the ones who lose most if barrels are

Left: The grave of smuggler Robert Trotman in Kinson churchyard near Bournemouth. The inscription reads: "To the memory of Robert Trotman late of Rond in the county of Wilts who was barbarously murdered on the shore near Poole the 24th March 1765.
A little tea one leaf I did not steal
For guiltless blood spilt I to God appeal
Put tea in one scale human blood in t'other
And think what tis to slay a human brother."

seized by the Revenue men. She makes the point to the preacher that the welfare of the village depends on the smuggling activity; she would be unable to look after her old, infirm mother if she stopped smuggling.

Hardy not only provides an accurate description of the mechanics of smuggling in 19th century Dorset, he also neatly summarises and explores the moral issues. The preacher, of course, disapproves of smuggling but still accompanies his love on nightly escapades to see that no harm befalls her. He is never tempted to turn informer and is not openly critical, even to members of his congregation whom he discovers in the smuggling gang! Naturally, a person in his position cannot marry someone involved in illegal activity, but all he demands is that she give it up. Her reasons for not doing so, despite the love she feels, not only involve the excitement that livens up an otherwise dull, rural existence but also her responsibility to the welfare of the villagers who depend on the illicit trade.

All these points applied to many Dorset villages and villagers in the late 18th and early 19th centuries. The taxes levied were unquestionably harsh and the distribution of wealth obscenely uneven. Most of the population would have had no moral qualms about cheating the Customs offices, indeed the welfare of thousands depended on smuggling activity. What Hardy's story doesn't reveal, however, is the increasing use of violence that was necessary for the smugglers to remain active. In "The Distracted Preacher" the villagers recover seized contraband and merely tie up the Excise men - no harm comes to them. This was not always the case in real life. Although law enforcement officers often offered little resistance to large gangs of smugglers, instances of violence increased and excise men were regularly threatened and intimidated.

In Kinson churchyard is the grave of the leader of a local smuggling gang, shot on the shore near Poole in 1765. The inscription implies a ruthless action by the Revenue men and it is clear the smugglers do not see smuggling tea they have bought as a crime. However, reports of the incident show that it was the smugglers who initiated the violence. Three Revenue men were injured before any shots were fired. Interestingly, two smugglers found themselves on the jury at the inquest which ruled that Trotman had been murdered; a clear indication that public sympathy rested firmly with the smugglers.

Smuggling Places

Christchurch, Bournemouth and Poole

In the 18th century Christchurch was not the gentle, well-trimmed resort we see today; it was an altogether rougher, wilder place. On his tour of Britain in the 1720s Daniel Defoe describes Christchurch as a "very inconsiderable, poor place, scarce worth seeing". No lucrative tourist trade supported the citizens of this ancient borough; to make ends meet most of the town was involved in smuggling.

A number of natural advantages encouraged this trade. Firstly there was an excellent harbour where goods could be safely unloaded. If you have stood on Mudeford Quay and watched the entrance to the harbour you cannot have failed to notice the strong currents that the rising and falling tide induces. The smugglers were usually expert sailors who knew the area well, to them the "Run" provided a way of losing the Revenue cutters who would not dare risk the treacherous harbour entrance. Secondly, access to the town on the landward side was via two bridges, easy to watch and guard if Revenue men were about. Finally, Christchurch is at the confluence of two rivers, the Stour and Avon; these provided important inland routes for the contraband.

Alongside the town, Hengistbury Head provided an ideal lookout station and the twin Iron Age dykes, built as defences across the neck of the headland over two thousand years ago, suited the smugglers perfectly as places to hide wagons and horses prior to a landing.

Left: The entrance to Christchurch Harbour at Mudeford Quay. Dangerous currents often deterred Revenue cutters from following the smugglers. Right: Hengistbury Head where the Iron Age dykes come down to the shore. Smugglers unloaded here then used the cover provided by the dykes.

On 14th July 1784 Mudeford was the scene of a famous battle between smugglers and a combined party of Revenue men and the Royal Navy. The sloop HMS Orestes was cruising the coast on the lookout for smugglers when she met two Revenue cutters and was informed of a smuggling operation going on at Mudeford. When she arrived a huge cargo of about 120 000 gallons of brandy and many tons of tea was already being unloaded on the beach near the modern car park. Hundreds of horses and carts were involved. Captain Ellis immediately launched two boats full of sailors armed to the teeth. As they approached the shore they were met by a volley of pistol and musket fire. The smugglers had dug themselves in on the beach and some retreated to the Haven Inn where they fired from windows. The fight may have gone on for many hours; the Revenue men secured the smugglers' luggers on the beach but the valuable cargo was safely taken away inland. In the end the smugglers made their escape and the King's men took their wounded back to ship. There was one fatality that day, William Allen, the sailing master of Orestes. It is not known if any of the smugglers were wounded.

The killing of William Allen led to an intensive hunt for the smugglers, but only one was brought to justice. George Coombs was subsequently hanged at Execution Dock on the Thames at Wapping and his body hung in chains at Haven Point as a warning.

Above: A view across to Bournemouth from Hengistbury Head. This is how all the coastline here would have looked in smuggling days.

Bournemouth may seem an unlikely place to have a smuggling history. Crowded with hotels, shops, entertainment complexes and thronged with holidaymakers at all times of the year, it is difficult to imagine boats landing surreptitiously and contraband being secreted away inland. Yet in the 18th century Bournemouth did not exist as we know it today; Daniel Defoe has nothing to say about it at all. Then it was a barren wilderness of heathland stretching all the way inland to Cranborne Chase. The broad bay stretched from Hengistbury Head to the Isle of Purbeck and had a gently sloping, sandy beach. Numerous little valleys known as "chines" or "bunnies" penetrate the sandy cliffs and provide route ways for goods landed on the beach. All in all it is difficult to imagine a more perfect location for the illicit trade.

Throughout the 18th and early 19th centuries thousands of barrels of brandy and packets of tea were landed on the beaches at places we know today as Bournemouth, Southbourne and Boscombe. Horses and carts took the goods inland into the deserted heathlands and across Cranborne Chase and the New Forest, ideal scenery for such clandestine activities. Many of the holidaymakers today strolling through the pleasure gardens behind Bournemouth pier are probably unaware of the secret convoys and bloody battles that were once commonplace here.

Many stories from these days have survived; some have been embellished to include the supernatural. At Southbourne, at the end of what is now Clifton Road, two young lovers were participants in a smuggling enterprise. The dashing young man was captain of the lugger trying to land in rough seas while his sweetheart stood as lookout on the cliffs. One or both seems to have acted in haste, for the swell was too great to attempt a landing near the dangerous rocks. The ship was lost with all on board and the devastated girl threw herself off the cliffs to join her lover. It is said that, on the anniversary of her death, she can be seen again throwing herself into the waves.

Around what is now Bournemouth pier in 1787 a smugglers' lugger was unloading brandy and tea when it was spotted by a Revenue cutter. An armed party was sent ashore and the smugglers ran off. However, they returned soon after with many more armed, mounted colleagues and a terrific fire-fight ensued. Despite a number of men being brought down as the Revenue men opened fire, the smugglers continued their attack and eventually regained their cargo. The leader of the Revenue men was savagely beaten. Eventually the gang's leader was caught, convicted and hanged at Newgate Prison.

Many people know that Poole has the second largest natural harbour in the world. Once a ship has navigated the narrow entrance there are dozens of creeks, inlets and beaches it can visit and islands it can hide behind. All this, of course, is perfect for the smuggler.

Poole Harbour from Lake

Poole in the 18th century was a large port; with its deep water harbour it could handle ocean going ships and saw many East Indiamen and ships plying the important trade with Newfoundland.

Poole was also a major Customs centre with the Custom House still standing on the quay. Customs lookouts were posted on Brownsea Island as well as the quay itself. Consequently smugglers had to be a great deal cleverer than at many places on the Dorset coast. So what made Poole a major smuggling centre?

Firstly, larger ships could use Poole. Although these carried legitimate cargoes, many had ample room for secret compartments at the bottom of their large holds. Secondly, the merchants themselves were involved in smuggling and many had tunnels constructed from their quays to secret hideaways in the town. Thus contraband could often be unloaded as simply as the legitimate cargo. Finally, many roads led away from Poole; those across the barren heathland were particularly useful to the smuggler.

Also, the Preventive Officers of Poole were notoriously corrupt. In 1788 a smuggling vessel was boarded and a detailed map was found showing the patrol areas of the Customs vessels. It had been written by the Deputy Controller at Poole! The Revenue cutter based at Poole made very few seizures compared to the one based at Southampton.

The increased use of violence was also a major factor and in the 1780s the situation was largely out of control. In 1786 a group

Left: Poole Custom House built in 1813 with a replica of the town beam used for weighing goods.
Above: The town quay, much different today than in the 18th century but perhaps the Customs officials have to be on the look out for different types of smuggling?

Above: The medieval bridge over the Avon in Fordingbridge that the Hawkhurst gang would have crossed.

of Poole smugglers openly, in daylight, carried away 400 casks of brandy with no one able or willing to try and stop them. In the same year a Poole surgeon attended 37 men who had been injured in one smuggling incident.

One of the most infamous of all smuggling incidents was centred around Poole in 1747 when, it seems, the Customs Service there was not yet as corrupt as it was to become later. A cargo of tea bought by the infamous Hawkhurst gang from Sussex was intercepted by the Poole Revenue cutter and brought to the Custom House on the quay. The gang gathered together a large, armed party and went to Poole to reclaim their cargo. They arrived at Poole, smashed open the vaults in the Custom House, loaded the tea onto their horses and began the slow march back to Sussex. All this was done without them being challenged at all!

They made a somewhat triumphant procession back to Hawkhurst, being given a rousing reception by the townsfolk of Fordingbridge in particular. There, one of the smugglers recognised a familiar face in the crowd, a man called Chater. Brazenly, he threw him a packet of tea as he marched along. Chater later read of the large reward attached to the capture of the gang and decided to turn informant. Whilst being escorted to Sussex by a Customs Officer named Galley they were captured by the Hawkhurst gang. The gruesome events that followed have been recounted many times. They involved both men being savagely beaten, dragged along by horses, Galley being buried alive and Chater mutilated with a knife then thrown down a well and finished off by dropping stones on him. These dreadful murders at last spurred the authorities to act. Seven of the murderers were eventually caught, tried and executed, followed by five more members of the gang. That was the end of the Hawkhurst gang.

The Isle of Purbeck

South of Poole Harbour lies the Isle of Purbeck, not a real island but nevertheless distinct and unique in character. Not to be outdone by the bigger urban centres of Poole and Christchurch, the inhabitants of Purbeck also had a prosperous and well organised smuggling industry. Once again the coastline provided its own natural benefits to the smugglers, but there were also some man-made bonuses.

Studland Bay, south of the entrance to Poole Harbour, is a marvellous gently sloping, sandy beach ideal for the landing of small smugglers' boats. Barrels could be sunk in the fine sand and the ample supply of seaweed provided additional cover. Behind the beach is the wild expanse of Studland Heath, perfect for convoys of men and horses to cross undetected. The goods would often be taken to small places on Poole Harbour, perhaps to be shipped out again

by boat as the roads out of Purbeck were well guarded. Overlooking Studland Bay is Handfast Point, high up on the chalk headland and an ideal lookout place. One famous smuggler of Studland was a lady called Jenny Gould. It's not clear what exactly her role was, probably an organiser of some sort, but local people also believed she was a witch, potentially a very useful attribute!

Just around the Chalk headland from Studland, Swanage too has a broad, sheltered bay and a gently sloping, sandy beach, ideal for landing and unloading small boats. In the 18th and 19th centuries it also had a busy quay where ships carrying Portland Stone would dock. Many of these had secret compartments where tea, brandy and other smuggled goods were stored and doubtless the many inns along the sea front were used to hide the contraband. All in all Swanage was a smuggler's heaven, so rife was the "trade" that when the Coastguard Service was formed in 1822 Swanage was the base for sixteen of its officers.

Westwards from Swanage the Purbeck coast is dominated by the Portland and Purbeck limestones. Dramatic cliffs are peppered with man made caves, tunnels and galleries where hardy men once cut and blasted one of the world's best building stones. Artificial quays were cut where stone was loaded onto barges and ferried to bigger ships offshore. Could there be a better place to smuggle goods ashore?

As is usual in the immediate hinterland of a smuggling coast, numerous places were used to store goods before they were shipped for sale and distribution. One such place in Purbeck was the church in the village of Langton Matravers. Some time in the 1790s a large shipment of brandy kegs was brought ashore and stored above the ceiling of the church. This was done without the knowledge of the

Left: The village of Studland on the Isle of Purbeck. The large, sheltered bay and gently sloping sandy beach made it an ideal place to land contraband.

Right: The dramatic coastline at Winspit. Quarrying works provided ideal hiding places!

Above: St. Aldhelm's chapel near Worth Matravers. Note the coastguard cottages behind.

vicar who might have been able to warn of the potential dangers of such a hiding place. As luck would have it, the ceiling gave way during a Sunday service, killing one of the congregation and injuring many more. Local legend says that the dreadful moment came just as the congregation was singing the line of a psalm which goes "And thy paths drop fatness"!

The village of Worth Matravers was a control centre for many local smuggling operations and one can imagine many of the stone cottages here regularly hiding a few casks of brandy or packets of tea before they were transported on to be sold. A number of paths meet here from the rocky coast where, by day, men cut and blasted the Portland Stone. Winspit is a good place to see the old quarry workings and huge caves and tunnels provided ideal places to store contraband before it was moved inshore. The smugglers' luggers would have used the quays that had been created for the barges to load stone - a very efficient use of resources!

Just west of Worth Matravers is St. Aldhelm's Head. There a disused Norman chapel dedicated to the saint made an excellent lookout for the smugglers trying to use Winspit or the lovely bay of Chapman's Pool to the west. It has been the site of a coastguard station for many years.

Kimmeridge is now famous for its geology and its underwater nature reserve. This beautiful bay attracts thousands of tourists but in the 18th century it was a favourite of the smuggler. Its

Above: Looking towards Gad Cliff and Brandy Bay from Kimmeridge.

gently sloping beach meant that it could be used in all weathers and once again a local landmark provided an excellent lookout. Clavel's Tower sits on the eastern headland of the bay; a folly erected by the Rev. John Clavel who was the squire of nearby Smedmore House. A small quay was built at Kimmeridge for the use of fishermen and boats which took the shale to France where it was used to make lamp oil. No doubt the smugglers found this equally useful. A lookout was certainly needed at Kimmeridge as the notorious ledges by the headland were very dangerous to shipping. Today the Smedmore Estate still owns Kimmeridge and it is difficult to imagine any significant smuggling going on here without the knowledge and probable involvement of the squire. This was probably true of many places along the Dorset coast and many rich landowners not only knew of and participated in the illegal trade but were the financiers and organisers behind the whole business.

Between Kimmeridge and Worbarrow Bay the Portland Limestone again forms the coastline. However it is not the horizontal layers that we see at Winspit. Here the limestone bedding planes are more upright, being the vertical limb of a giant fold created by great earth movements. The result is the high, sheer rock face known as Gad Cliff. Beneath is the gentle sweep of Brandy Bay - no great insight is required to understand where this name came from! The beach can only be accessed by sea, but it was ideal for the smugglers' shallow bottomed boats to draw up on and their cargo could be hauled up the cliffs by rope, pulled by colleagues on top. From here a path leads down to the now ruined but atmospheric village of Tyneham, where no doubt it was often hidden until it could be distributed.

The route from Gad Cliff was not the only way that smuggled goods came through Tyneham. From the village a path leads down to Worbarrow Bay, one of the most picturesque bays in Dorset, its appeal enhanced by the lack of commercialisation [Tyneham and Worbarrow are still on army ranges]. One report tells how, in 1719, five smugglers' luggers unloaded together at Worbarrow with the goods being sold openly on the beach as if it was a market! There is another smuggling tale from Worbarrow, that of a lone smuggler who was surprised by Revenue men one night. Trying to run away, he found himself trapped against the sheer cliffs with no escape. It is said the Revenue men drove him into the sea where he was stoned to death. Legend says his ghostly cries can still be heard on dark nights.

Above: A ruined coastguard cottage sits on the edge of Worbarrow Bay.

As you walk down to the beach at Worbarrow you pass two ruined coastguard cottages, built in the early 19th century to deter and apprehend smugglers using this bay. In the 1851 Census, taken at a time when smuggling had been severely curtailed by the introduction of the Coastguard Service and changes to excise duties, out of 37 households recorded 10 had a member of the Coastguard as head. This illustrates how endemic smuggling had become in the previous century and how important the government finally realised it was to deal with it.

A little further along the coast from Worbarrow is one of the most famous harbours in all of Britain, Lulworth Cove. As might be expected, Lulworth too had a thriving smuggling industry. Although it provides an exceptionally safe harbour, the drawback for ships on illegal business is the narrow entrance. Perhaps this is why smuggling at Lulworth involved large gangs who were unafraid of the Revenue men and often brazen enough to go about their business in the open. Almost the whole village was involved in one way or another. Apparently even the stately Lulworth Castle, home of the local squire, was put to use, with servants signalling from upstairs windows to alert ships. One smuggling tale from Lulworth tells of two Revenue men caught watching a gang of smugglers. They were disarmed, bound and hung from the cliff while the smugglers finished their work. They were then cut free and sent on their way.

Above: The sheltered harbour at Lulworth Cove.

Above: The Smugglers' Inn at Osmington Mills.

The smugglers of Lulworth were not always that merciful. In 1832 the Chief Coastguard Officer was caught by Lulworth smugglers, severely beaten and thrown off the cliffs near Durdle Door. He was Lieutenant Thomas Edward Knight and is buried in a cemetery in Weymouth; he was 42.

In Thomas Hardy's story "The Distracted Preacher", Lulworth is the scene for the landing of the smuggled brandy kegs. Here is a detailed description of what a real smuggling operation would have been like, with large numbers of men involved, secret hiding places carefully arranged, lookouts on the shore and a well organised landing party.

Weymouth, Portland and Chesil Bank

West from Lulworth Cove the high cliffs of the Chalk give way to softer rocks which form a coastline prone to landslips. The next good harbour is in the shelter of the small promontory at Osmington Mills. Here the well known Smugglers' Inn leaves no doubt that this was another place the illegal trade was practised! The inn dates from the 13th century and was formerly called The Crown. Its present name was used unofficially from the late 18th century, only being formally adopted in the 1970s. The Crown was the base for a famous smuggler known as "French Peter".

In the late 18th and early 19th century Weymouth profited from being a centre for privateers, pirates licensed to attack and plunder French shipping. This was also the reign of King George III who made Weymouth famous by patronising it as a place for rest and relaxation at a time when the concept of a seaside resort was not really established. When he visited the king brought thousands of people with him; thus Weymouth was transformed into a busy cosmopolitan area. These visitors provided an insatiable market for smuggled goods, encouraging the town to become a smuggling centre also, although a strangely seasonal one, as when the king left thousands left with him!

Smuggling operations in Weymouth were "encouraged" by an indolent and incompetent Customs service. Perhaps many experienced seamen who might have been tempted to make a living by intercepting smugglers saw the life of a privateer as more rewarding. Many local entrepreneurs financed the fitting out of ships for privateers and made a handsome return on their investment. The Black Dog Inn in St. Mary Street was an inn much frequented by smugglers. A Customs officer was brutally beaten to death here when he tried to arrest a smuggler who was hiding in the inn.

Joining Portland to the mainland is one of England's most well known natural features, Chesil Bank, an eighteen mile long stretch of shingle formed by storm waves dragging pebbles eastwards along the coast. Behind the bank are the calm waters of the Fleet, a place famously associated with smuggling thanks to the fictional story "Moonfleet" by J. Meade Falkner. This was an area with many advantages for the smuggler, particularly one who knew the area well. Since the pebbles grade in size from west to east, becoming gradually smaller, an experienced local sailor could determine where he was on the beach in the dead of night simply from the size of the pebbles he encountered. A landing party could then haul the barrels over the bank and sink them in the Fleet for collection later.

There were disadvantages for the smuggler too; the currents off Chesil Bank are often strong and dangerous, storms can be devastating here. Many ships have been wrecked on the bank and it has been known for storm waves to lift ships clean over the bank into the Fleet. In 1824 the village of Fleet was destroyed by a great storm, waves breached the bank early in the morning and seven large fishing boats were swept far inland. In 1822 a local fisherman was imprisoned for "unlawfully making a light on the coast", suggesting he was involved in the cruel and ruthless crime of wrecking, where ships were deliberately led onto dangerous shores by putting lights in the wrong positions.

In 1717 a report from the Collector of Customs at Weymouth notes that three officers investigating a reported smuggling operation on Chesil Bank were met by an armed gang of around thirty men and were driven off. This suggests that, even at this early stage, smuggling around the Fleet was well organised. Between 1815 and 1825, 24 local men were jailed for smuggling but not one was from the village of Fleet itself. Perhaps Falkner picked on the wrong village when he wrote his story although it is more likely the men of Fleet were simply too good to be caught!

At the western end of the Fleet lies Abbotsbury, home of the famous Swannery. The village was well known for both smugglers and wreckers and no doubt the ancient tithe barn was used as a storage place for contraband and St. Catherine's chapel on the hill made an excellent lookout. Today the Smugglers' Barn at the Children's Farm has full scale replicas of a smuggling lugger and a Revenue cutter.

On the hills around Abbotsbury are numerous Bronze Age burial barrows. Many of these were excavated by farmers who, after removing bones, beakers and anything likely to be valuable, used the resulting cavities to hide contraband. Such places have

Below: The picturesque village of Abbotsbury. The "Smugglers' Barn" is on the far right of the picture.

often encouraged ghostly stories which would have been fostered by the smugglers eager to keep prying eyes away! The control centre of smuggling in Abbotsbury was the Ship Inn, now known as the Ilchester Arms.

Burton Bradstock to Lyme Regis

Burton Bradstock was another major smuggling centre and the Dove Inn was the place where they met. One of the most famous of all smugglers, Isaac Gulliver, used Burton Bradstock as a base and even went to the extreme length of buying Eggardon Hill a little way inland because it made a good lookout and signal location. Farmers in the surrounding countryside planted small groups of trees on hill tops so they could be used as markers by smuggling ships.

The harbour at West Bay is still a busy little place. In the 18th and 19th centuries many boats exported rope for which neighbouring Bridport was famous. Like Lulworth there is a narrow entrance to the harbour and the smuggling here had to be done secretly by way of hidden compartments in ships that were legitimately trading in the harbour. The little town of Chideock with its neighbouring beach at Seatown was the province of a well known smuggling gang led by "the Colonel", an enigmatic figure who was probably a retired army officer. He was an expert organiser and ensured the goods were safely taken by pack horses to inland markets such as Beaminster, Chard and Yeovil. It is said that

Right: The busy little harbour at West Bay near Bridport.

the entire population of Chideock was involved in smuggling which they carried on using a relatively narrow stretch of coastline between Seatown and Charmouth. They were blessed with one of the best lookout positions imaginable, the 600 feet high Golden Cap.

Lyme Regis sits on the border with Devon and is the last of our Dorset smuggling centres. With its ancient, artificial harbour, the Cobb, Lyme was a well known and important port on the south coast. Perhaps more famous for its part in the disastrous rebellion by James, Duke of Monmouth, it too has its smuggling history. It was here that Isaac Gulliver's men unloaded their goods in full view of Customs officials.

Although our story ends here in one of Dorset's most historic and scenic towns, smugglers used virtually the whole of the south coast to land their cargoes. Nor is it just the coastal towns and villages that have a smuggling heritage, many inland towns were famous as holding locations or markets for the contraband. Finally, remember, as you enjoy walking the glorious scenery on the South West Coast Path, what its origins were. Uniquely among Britain's long distance paths, it began as a working route for the Riding Officers of the Revenue Service and later the Coastguards as they scoured the shoreline looking out for the smugglers' luggers and the trains of pack horses scurrying away with their brandy and tea. Naturally it was equally useful for the smugglers as they moved from place to place to signal to their comrades out at sea!

Right: The harbour from the Cobb at Lyme Regis.

Some Famous Smugglers

....

Isaac Gulliver

Perhaps the most well known of all Dorset smugglers was Isaac Gulliver. A resourceful, organised and energetic character, he became fabulously wealthy over a long career and had hundreds of men working for him. Known as the "gentle smuggler", it is said he never killed a man and instilled great discipline into his men.

Isaac was born in Wiltshire in 1745 and was active in the golden age of smuggling, before the Coastguard Service had been formed. He made his base in the village of Longham near Poole and soon had 15 ships carrying his goods across the Channel from France and the Channel Islands. These landed at various places around Bournemouth, particularly the chines or small wooded valleys where streams entered the sea and the mouth of the River Bourne where the central gardens are today. From there long trains of pack horses would take the goods up the valleys and onto the wild heathland beyond, to be secreted in numerous places in the hinterland. In 1780 Gulliver moved to Kinson where he built himself a huge house with the profits from his lucrative trade. It was an imposing structure with mock fortifications and many secret rooms for hiding contraband. It is claimed that a vast network of tunnels was built under Kinson with storage chambers under virtually every large house. The centre of the network was the parish church, which not only provided

Left: Kinson Church was a nerve centre for local smugglers. A number are buried in the graveyard. Contraband was stored in the tower.

Above: Eggardon Hill makes an ideal smuggler's lookout. Ships bringing contraband would be able to see pre-arranged signals from the hill telling them where was safe to land. Isaac Gulliver also planted trees on the hill so that his ships would be able to navigate more easily and recognise their signals.

excellent storage places but was also useful as a lookout tower, exactly as happens in Hardy's "The Distracted Preacher".

Gradually Isaac Gulliver extended his domain further west and in 1776 he bought a farm at the foot of Eggardon Hill in west Dorset. This spectacular Iron Age hillfort has amazing views out into the Channel and Isaac had a circle of trees planted to guide incoming ships. His ships landed at many places from Burton Bradstock to Lyme Regis, often unloading in daylight at harbours and with little concern for the Customs officials. By this time Gulliver had become extremely rich and was probably now using bribery rather than stealth to ply his trade. He invested in a number of properties all of which, no doubt, were equipped to hide smuggled goods.

Isaac Gulliver's career seems full of contradictions. On the one hand there are stories of him evading capture by Revenue men by arranging his fake funeral, hiding in empty brandy barrels and dashing across the heath on his famous white horse, yet he also seems to have enjoyed immunity from capture and prosecution.

There is no doubt that as his business flourished many officials would have accepted bribes from him but there are also stories of him passing information he had learned about French invasion plans or troop movements to the naval authorities. During this time the threat of French invasion was very real and it may be that Gulliver was too useful to apprehend.

In 1782 Gulliver surprisingly applied for and won the King's pardon and announced that he was going to pursue a career selling fine wines and spirits to the gentry. This he did very successfully, although the very reasonable prices he charged led many to believe that he had not paid much in the way of customs duties!

Gulliver finally settled in a large house in Wimborne and died there in 1822 at the age of 77. He left a considerable fortune and much property, some of it to a variety of charities, further enhancing his reputation as the "gentle smuggler".

Above: Burton Beach at Burton Bradstock. Burton Bradstock was a major smuggling centre in Lyme Bay with smugglers using the Dove Inn as a rendezvous.

Left: Looking over The Fleet towards Portland. St. Catherine's chapel is in the middle foreground.

Roger Ridout

Not all famous smugglers were involved in daring escapades at sea or on the coast on dark, moonless nights: some undertook the more prosaic work of shipping the goods inland to the various towns and markets where they could be sold. If anything this required even more skill and patience. Long convoys of horses or mules were often involved and journeys took a considerable time, giving ample opportunities for Revenue men to intercept. One such Dorset smuggler who excelled at the arrangements for the dispersal of contraband was Roger Ridout.

Ridout was born in Shroton [also known as Iwerne Courtenay] in 1736. He became a miller, living in nearby Okeford Fitzpaine where he is buried. He seems to have specialised in bringing brandy kegs up from Lulworth Cove and it is likely he worked in collaboration with Isaac Gulliver. Numerous stories have grown up about Roger Ridout, some of which seem unlikely to say the least. Others, such as escaping from houses using sheets tied together may have more truth. Perhaps this is just a confirmation of

how successful Ridout was. He must have been well known locally and have "employed" many men. His contribution to the local economy probably made him very popular and, like Gulliver, he was seen to have outwitted the Revenue on many occasions. All this would have given him a larger than life reputation.

However, he does seem to have spent some time in Dorchester gaol which gave rise to another story; that his devoted wife made a round trip of forty miles on foot concealing a bladder of brandy which he enjoyed via a tube through the bars of his cell!

Lewis Tregonwell

Lewis Tregonwell is generally regarded as being the founder of the modern resort town of Bournemouth. Tregonwell was a very successful Dorset gentleman. He lived at Cranborne Lodge and was an army captain. During the tense years that England feared an invasion by Napoleon's army across the Channel, Captain Tregonwell was put in charge of the Dorset Rangers and given the job of patrolling the coast. In addition to looking out for French ships the job entailed looking out for smugglers.

In 1810 the threat of invasion had receded and Tregonwell had retired. His wife was not very well and while visiting the coast she fell in love with the area around the Bourne stream and Tregonwell decided to build her a house there. He built further, smaller houses for his staff and followed this up by building more villas which he let out as holiday homes. People were, by this time, beginning to realise the benefits of sea air and slowly but surely Bournemouth grew to the popular resort it still is today. Tregonwell's original house has since metamorphosed into the Royal Exeter Hotel.

So what has all this to do with smuggling? Well, it seems Tregonwell had a loyal butler named Symes, for whom he had a lodge built at Bournemouth. When the lodge was demolished in the 1930s a secret chamber was found underneath it. Symes' family

Opposite: "Landfall" © Richard Platt, "Smugglers' Britain" 2006
Getting the contraband ashore was only the first stage. Convoys had to be organised to take the goods to markets inland. Teams of horses and donkeys were often used and the wild heathlands of Dorset provided ideal territory across which to travel undetected.

were well known smugglers in the Cranborne area. Could it be that Tregonwell was involved in smuggling all the time, perhaps with his faithful butler looking after the day to day running of the operation? Certainly Tregonwell's house was in an ideal position as a lookout! Why would he choose to build a house in what was a fairly wild and undeveloped area? Also, Tregonwell's main residence, Cranborne Lodge, lay on one of the main smuggling routes north from Bournemouth. Geoffrey Morley in his book "Smuggling in Hampshire and Dorset 1700-1850", suggests Tregonwell may even have been in league with Isaac Gulliver; it would certainly explain why the Dorset Rangers never caught Gulliver!

Why would a man like Tregonwell have been involved in smuggling? He was independently wealthy and well respected. Perhaps for a man who had led an eventful and active life retirement at Bournemouth would have been a little dull. Maybe the excitement and adventure of smuggling was too much to resist?

Further reading and bibliography:

Smuggling in Hampshire and Dorset 1700-1850
by Geoffrey Morley

Smugglers' Britain by Richard Platt - www.smuggling.co.uk

www.dorsetsmugglers.co.uk

The Distracted Preacher by Thomas Hardy

www.burtonbradstock.org.uk